D0570849

INVENTIONS
THAT CHANGED
THE WORLD

JOHANNES GUTENBERG

and the PRINTING PRESS

Louise Spilsbury

PowerKiDS
press

NEW YORK

Published in 2016 by **The Rosen Publishing Group**
29 East 21st Street, New York, NY 10010

Produced for Rosen by Calcium

Editors for Calcium: Harriet McGregor and Sarah Eason
Designers: Jessica Moon and Paul Myerscough
Picture Research: Harriet McGregor

Picture credits: Cover: Getty Images: GeorgiosArt (fg); Shutterstock: pavila (bkgd). Insides:
Dreamstime: Cybervam 11, Ingriddeelen 13, Georgios Kollidas 5, 28, Pius Lee 17, Mineria6
18–19, Philippehalle 25, Photographerlondon 27, Dariusz Sas 14t, Spaceheater 21, Zlikovec 12;
Shutterstock: Roberto Castillo 9, Gio.tto 4, Morphart Creation 6, 23, Mikhail Pogosov 14–15,
Pressmaster 26–27, Tupungato 7; Wikimedia Commons: 10, 19, 22.

Cataloging-in-Publication Data
Spilsbury, Louise.
Johannes Gutenberg and the printing press / by Louise Spilsbury.
p. cm. — (Inventions that changed the world)
Includes index.
ISBN 978-1-5081-4631-5 (pbk.)
ISBN 978-1-5081-4632-2 (6-pack)
ISBN 978-1-5081-4633-9 (library binding)
1. Gutenberg, Johann, — 1397?-1468 — Juvenile literature.
2. Printers — Germany — Biography — Juvenile literature.
3. Printers — Germany — Biography — Juvenile literature.
I. Spilsbury, Louise. II. Title.
Z126.Z7 S65 2016
686.2092—d23

Manufactured in the United States of America
CPSIA Compliance Information: Batch #BW16PK: For Further Information contact Rosen Publishing, New York, New York at 1-800-237-9932

CONTENTS

THE POWER OF THE PRINTING PRESS

Much of Johannes Gutenberg's life is a mystery. We are uncertain about his actual birth date, and the portrait shown right was based on guesswork about his appearance. One thing we know for sure is that Johannes Gutenberg created an incredible invention that changed the world forever: the printing press.

CHANGING THE WORLD

A printing press is a machine that transfers images and letters to paper using ink. It might not sound as exciting as a rocket or a computer, but Johannes's invention changed the world in a way that few other inventions could ever claim to do. Most of us take printed materials for granted, but imagine what our world would be like without them. We would not have books, magazines, posters, catalogs, comics, or newspapers. And even though many printed materials are now found online, printing is just as important today as it has ever been. The printing press allows us to share large amounts of information quickly, and in huge numbers. In fact, the printing press is so important that many people claim it is one of the most important inventions in history.

Printing books like these in great numbers only became possible as a result of Johannes's great invention.

Johannes's Success

Johannes was not the first person to come up with the idea of **movable type**, but he was the first to make it successful. In China, around AD 600, an early printing technique involved carving words into wooden blocks and pressing them onto paper. Later, in China and Korea, another technique used movable wooden **characters** to create **type** on a page. These techniques did not catch on because the languages of China and Korea used tens of thousands of different characters. It took too long to set a page. By comparison, European languages have far fewer letters, so were ideal for movable type.

EARLY YEARS

Johannes was born around 1398 (the exact date is unknown), in the German city of Mainz. He was the youngest son of five children born to the nobleman Friele Gensfleisch zur Laden, and his second wife, Else Wyrich, who was the daughter of a storekeeper. During the 1300s, names were not passed on from father to son and Johannes took the name Gutenberg from one of his father's houses.

GROWING UP

As a boy, it is probable that Johannes went to one of the local religious schools in Mainz, as did most of the other children from wealthy families. After that, it is thought he went to the University of Erfurt, where two of his cousins studied. Johannes's father oversaw the archbishop's **mint** in the main square of Mainz, across from the cathedral and just two minutes from the family home. As he grew up, Johannes must have seen and learned a lot about the goldsmith and blacksmith trades by watching his father do business.

In the 1400s, Mainz was an important trading center.

MAKING MONEY

The archbishop of Mainz was very powerful and controlled the mint, where coins were made. Johannes's father supplied the mint with metal to be made into coins, worked on different types of coins, and even sat in on forgery cases. When he was young, Johannes must have been fascinated as he watched workers at the mint stamping and engraving images onto coins.

Wealth and Ambition

At the time when Johannes was growing up in Mainz, his home town was one of the wealthiest and most important cities along the Rhine River. Mainz was a vibrant trading center because it is the meeting point of two rivers: the Rhine and the Main. From there, goods were delivered and collected between Germany and the rest of Europe. As Johannes was growing up in Mainz, he quickly became aware that men with ideas and ambition could make money and fame for themselves.

The archbishop of Mainz ruled the province, but noblemen like Johannes's father also had a say in running the town. Sometimes, this caused disputes with smaller traders and **guildsmen**, who wanted more control and resented the taxes that the nobles took from them. For a while in the 1420s, the guildsmen had the upper hand and sent some noble families away. The Gutenbergs left Mainz during the late 1420s, and eventually settled in the city of Strasbourg, 150 miles (241 km) away.

This is the city of Mainz today. An entire museum in the city is dedicated to Johannes and his work.

WORKING IN METAL

Whatever subjects Johannes excelled in at school and university, his real interest lay in working with metal. In the 1430s, he was still living in Strasbourg, and although he had been engaged to a young woman from that city, the engagement had broken off and Johannes was unmarried. Both of his parents had died, so it was up to Johannes to make a living and care for himself. His parents had left him enough inheritance money to pay for a house in which to live, but Johannes was ambitious and he wanted to make a great career for himself.

A BUDDING BUSINESSMAN

In the mid 1400s, Strasbourg was a big, bustling city with 25,000 residents and many thriving businesses. At first, Johannes dabbled in different ventures. He tried his hand at developing a new technique for polishing gemstones, and later set out to make a successful business selling metal objects that he made himself, such as fine gold jewelry and metal souvenirs. He sold them to visitors in his local cathedral. Gradually, Johannes became more and more skilled at metalwork. In 1437, he believed he had discovered a winning moneymaking scheme: **pilgrim** mirrors.

MAKING MIRRORS

Every year, pilgrims came to Strasbourg to attend a religious event during which famous relics were put on show. Johannes took out loans to buy the materials and equipment that he and his fellow metalworkers needed to make small, decorated metal frames of a tin **alloy** in different shapes. A mirror was attached to the top of these frames, with small clips so that pilgrims could pin the decorative mirrors to their hats or clothes. Unfortunately, in 1439, the pilgrimage was canceled because there was an outbreak of the **plague**. Johannes was left with piles of mirrors that he could not sell and many loans that he could not pay back.

The plague was a terrible disease that killed millions of people. Cities took measures, such as canceling festivals, to try to stop the disease from spreading. This caused Johannes many financial problems.

Pilgrim Mirrors

Pilgrims bought mirrors because they believed the mirrors could catch the healing power of holy relics on display at religious festivals. They hoped to keep the power for luck or to share with relatives. Convex mirrors were thought to be especially effective because the curved surface reflected a greater area.

THE BIG IDEA

After the failure of his pilgrim mirrors, it was time for Johannes to come up with another moneymaking scheme. He was fascinated by new technologies and spent his time with a group of men who worked on inventions and were constantly seeking new ideas. Eventually, another religious product gave Johannes the inspiration he badly needed.

A PAINSTAKING PROCESS

In the 1400s, there was a market for paper pages of religious messages. In Europe, most of these pages and any books available were written by **scribes**, who had to copy page after page by hand. Most scribes were **monks**. It was their job to copy religious texts as an act of worship, but some scribes were young men working in universities, too. It was a painstakingly slow job. Even the best scribes could only complete a few pages each day, and it took yet more time for artists to draw images or patterns on the pages. Most books were bibles or other religious texts, and were usually owned only by monasteries, colleges, or very rich people. Families that owned books usually only owned one: the Bible.

Monks working as scribes worked in a special room in a monastery, called a *scriptorium*.

MAKING A DIFFERENCE

There were other problems with handwritten bibles and texts. Not only were they expensive because they took so long to make, but scribes often made mistakes. This led to confusion and disagreements between different Church groups about whose version was correct. Johannes must have wondered whether there was a way to make hundreds of copies of exactly the same page, or perhaps even of the same bible, for Christians everywhere to read and follow.

The kind of paper used by scribes was called **vellum**. This fine, expensive parchment was made from the skin of a calf.

Monks' Manuscripts

Scribes did most of their work early in the day when the light was good. It was too dangerous to use candles in a room full of expensive vellum and valuable manuscripts. In a scriptorium, scribes worked in total silence. They carefully measured and marked out their pages and then patiently copied the text from another book. Later, an artist called an illuminator would add art and patterns to the page, which is why they were known as **illuminated manuscripts**.

WORKING IN SECRET

Johannes began work on his next project in total secrecy. People saw him leaving and entering his large, very private house in Strasbourg and taking delivery of interesting looking parcels, but no one knew for certain what was going on behind those closed doors. It was as though Johannes knew he had stumbled on an idea that could change the world, and he did not want to risk someone stealing it!

RESEARCH

Johannes did not invent his printing press overnight. At first, he spent his time researching various other methods of printing, and testing out ideas of his own. To date, most previous attempts at printing had been basic. People cut letters or images onto blocks of wood that were then dipped in or brushed with ink and stamped or pressed onto paper. Although this method was used in China and Korea, it was really only used in the West to print playing cards. At the mint, Johannes had seen coins with images on them being cut from a machine and he knew that if he could use blocks cut with letters that were pressed by a machine, he could speed up the printing process and produce a lot of copies of texts in a short time.

> Before Johannes's invention, people carved wooden letters like these to stamp words onto paper.

From Old to New

Some people think that Johannes may have adapted some old farming technology to make his new printing press invention. He grew up in an area of Germany where people had long been making wine by pressing grapes for the juice, using a screw-type wine press. This device had a handle that turned to force a flat plate down onto fruit to squeeze out the juice. This type of press was also used to squeeze oil from olives and press water out of cloth, so Johannes would have often seen it in use. Why not, then, use this old, simple technology to do something entirely new?

LOOKING FOR LOANS

One problem Johannes faced was money. To cover his own expenses and to pay for the materials and equipment he needed for his work, he needed money. So he borrowed large amounts of it from a few investors who he let in on his secret. As his ideas grew, so did his need for cash. By 1448, Johannes had moved back to Mainz, and by 1449, he had borrowed a substantial amount of money from a businessman and moneylender named Johann Fust.

The invention of the printing press owed much to the ancient wine and olive presses of the Mediterranean area.

THE PRINTING PRESS

It took years for Johannes to perfect his printing invention. Using a press for printing was one of his most inspired ideas. Another was having the notion of **casting** metal type to print onto paper.

METAL MOVABLE TYPE

Instead of using woodblocks with letters, designs, or words carved onto them to print, Johannes decided to use metal instead. He made individual metal blocks for each letter or punctuation symbol he wanted to use, and he made many copies of each one. These metal block letters could be arranged into a **printing frame** to create words and sentences on a surface that could be printed from. The metal letters were called movable type because they could be moved and reused over and over to print words and sentences on a page. Each page could be printed in the press as many times as necessary.

Johannes was the first person to make movable pieces of type from metal. The metal he used was an alloy or mix of metals including lead, tin, and antimony.

MAKING TYPE

Johannes made hard steel tools with letter shapes at the end. He hammered the tools into soft copper to make letter-shaped **molds**. Earlier in his life he had seen a similar process in which coin makers made sticks with images on one end that could be pressed into soft metal. This technique was used to make the molds into which silver and gold were poured to make coins. For his press, Johannes cast metal type by pouring hot, liquid metal into the molds and leaving it to cool and harden. This method was quick and relatively easy, so using it meant all sorts of different characters or letters could be cast.

A New Printer's Ink

Johannes had to find a new ink to use in his press. In the early 1400s, printing ink was water-based, which was useless because it was thin and simply ran off metal type. Instead, Johannes developed a thick, sticky kind of ink based on the oil paints used by artists at the time. This ink stuck much more easily to the metal type. Johannes's ink contained sulfur and metals such as copper and lead, and was deep black and glossy. It was unusual, but of a very high quality. It was designed to print evenly and make the words that it printed stay visible for a very long time.

The challenge for Johannes was to design a printing press that could be used to print the black text for books as beautiful as this one.

HOW THE PRINTING PRESS WORKS

At last, Johannes's printing press was finished. It was built from a wooden frame with metal plates and it was operated by hand. The machine was sturdy and well-built so that it would be able to withstand repeated use.

USING THE PRINTING PRESS

To use the printing press, the first job was to make up each page of text by arranging individual letters of type in a type tray or frame. Together, the type blocks formed words and sentences, but each letter of metal type was a mirror image. The type also had to be laid, or set, backward in a frame, from right to left. The page was set in reverse so that it would read correctly, and from left to right, when it was printed.

Next, the frame was fitted into the metal bed of the press and the page of metal type was covered with ink, either by hand or with a brush. A sheet of paper or vellum was made slightly damp and then placed over the type and frame. When the handle was turned, the large screw of the press turned and brought down a heavy block of flat, smooth wood called the plate. This plate pushed tightly down and applied an even pressure onto the type and ink before being released. The words appeared on the paper correctly as a result of the reversed blocks, and the printing process was complete.

The Word Is...

Some religious people complained because the printing press was based on ancient wine presses, but Johannes remarked:

"Yes, it is a press, certainly, but a press from which shall flow in inexhaustible streams, the most abundant and most marvelous liquor that has ever flowed to relieve the thirst of men! Through it, God will spread His Word. A spring of truth shall flow from it: like a new star it shall scatter the darkness of ignorance, and cause a light heretofore unknown to shine among men."

Some traditional wooden book printing presses can still be seen in museums around the world today.

THE FIRST PRINTS

Johannes's press was a major breakthrough. Although it could still take a worker a whole day to fill one tray to make one page of text, once that type tray was done, it could be used many times to make many copies of the same page. Then, the individual metal type pieces could be reset for other pages. For the first time in history, books could be printed in great numbers in a short space of time, or mass-produced. This dramatically reduced the number of people needed to make a book, and therefore the cost of creating it, too.

PRINTING FOR PAYMENT

From around 1450, Johannes was using the printing press to do print jobs for payment. With his new invention, it was possible to print 42 lines of text at once. Before trying his hand at printing a long book, Johannes began by printing single sheets of paper and small books. Historians believe that the first things he printed were a German poem, a *Türkenkalender*, which was a warning against a possible invasion from Turkish forces, some school books of Latin grammar, and some Catholic letters of indulgence.

Religion was hugely important in the 1400s and many of Johannes's early prints were of Christian texts.

An indulgence was like a certificate signed by the **pope**. People could take the letter to their Church to show a priest as proof that they had the right to have their sins forgiven. Before the printing press, thousands of identical letters of indulgence had to be written out by hand. Now, they could be printed and produced for a much lower price. For Johannes, printing indulgences would have been an important source of money, which he greatly needed after investing so much for so long in his project.

The Word Is...

In March 1455, the future pope, Pius II, wrote about his admiration for Johannes's invention in a letter to an important Church leader:

"All that has been written to me about that marvelous man seen at Frankfurt is true. I have not seen complete bibles but only a number of quires [a set of 24 sheets of paper] of various books of the Bible. The script was very neat and legible, not at all difficult to follow. Your grace would be able to read it without effort, and indeed without glasses."

This image from 1500 shows the sale of letters of indulgence. When Johannes started selling his first printed letters of indulgence, he must have thought his financial worries were over at last.

THE GUTENBERG BIBLE

Johannes's first large-scale project was printing a bible. The famous *Gutenberg Bible*, as we know it today, was printed in around 1455. It was the first time the Bible had been mass-produced and would eventually become available for people outside of the Church to read. Before the *Gutenberg Bible*, bibles were highly expensive and rare, and could take up to a year for a priest to produce.

A PRINTING SUCCESS

The *Gutenberg Bible* is decorated with hundreds of two-color initial letters and delicate borders that Gutenberg printed using a smart new technique that required inking a single metal block several times. Each of the bibles contained more than 1,280 pages. Although no one knows exactly how many copies were printed, it is thought that Johannes planned to print around 160, but actually printed about 180 copies when he realized there was a great demand for them.

PAPER AND VELLUM

Around 135 copies were printed on paper and about 45 were printed on vellum, which was much more expensive. The skin of about 170 calves would have been required for each copy of the Bible printed on vellum! Although we do not know what the price of this original batch of bibles was, we do know that many of the copies were bought by wealthy churches and monasteries. There are only about 20 complete copies of the *Gutenberg Bible* left intact today. One of these bibles is likely worth around $30 million!

The Word Is...

Johannes wanted to make the Bible available to all. He explained:

"Religious truth is imprisoned in a small number of manuscript books which confine instead of spread the public treasure. Let us break the seal which seals up holy things and give wings to Truth in order that she may win every soul that comes into the world by her word no longer written at great expense by hands easily palsied, but multiplied like the wind by an untiring machine."

This is a page from a magnificent *Gutenberg Bible* printed in around 1455.

COURTROOM DRAMA

Johannes had finally achieved success, but unfortunately he was unable to enjoy his newfound good luck for long. Over the years, Johannes had borrowed a great deal of money to bring his dream to reality. Now, he was going to pay a heavy price for that debt.

FIGHTS WITH FUST

In 1455, Johannes found himself caught up in a bitter dispute with the wealthy moneylender, Johann Fust. Fust demanded that Johannes repay him all the money he borrowed, plus interest, claiming that Johannes had not used the funds as they had agreed. Johannes had received a loan of 800 florins (a medieval form of currency) from Fust in 1449, for printing equipment, and between 1452 and 1453, another 800 florins to print books and start producing the Bible. It is thought that Fust had grown frustrated that instead of printing more bibles quickly to make money as soon as possible, Johannes was more interested in producing absolutely perfect copies.

When Johannes could not pay back the debt, Fust took the case to the archbishop's court.

Some people believe that Johann Fust (right) and Peter Schoeffer, who later became Fust's son-in-law, conspired together to take control of Johannes's printing presses.

At the time when Johannes had taken the loan from Fust, he had agreed to use his printing equipment as security, meaning that if his invention failed, Fust would be able to make some of his money back from selling that equipment. This proved to be Johannes's downfall. After a heated dispute, the court decided in favor of Fust. Johannes was told to hand over the printing workshop and half of all the bibles that had already been printed to Fust. Johannes's great invention had been snatched from him, just as he was about to benefit from its success at long last.

This engraving shows workers operating an early printing press like that created by Johannes. The loss of his printing press was a cruel blow to Johannes after his many years of hard work.

Fust First

Fust took over Johannes's printing workshop and continued to run it with Peter Schoeffer, who had been one of Johannes's trusted workers. In 1457, the Fust–Schoeffer printing workshop became the first in Europe to bring out a book displaying the printer's name and date. It was a book of psalms called the *Mainz Psalter*, but it made no mention nor gave any credit to Johannes for inventing the printing press used to produce it.

LATER YEARS

It is not hard to imagine how Johannes felt after losing his printing press and business to Fust. Johannes had spent around 15 years of his life, off and on, experimenting with different metals, working, and struggling to pay for the equipment and time he needed to develop his printing press. Now it was all gone, and it seemed that Fust was determined that no one would ever know that it was Johannes who had invented the printing press.

HARD TIMES

Johannes was broke and in serious financial trouble. Luckily, he had held on to or started up a small printing workshop to try to make some money. This was nothing like the busy, successful workshop he had lost. Now, he mainly made small printed items that were produced quickly and cheaply, such as medical calendars and leaflets. It is also believed that he supplied the type for a bible in the town of Bamberg in around 1459, but his name never appeared on any books he had a part in producing, so it is hard to be certain. However, these products were far removed from the quality product Johannes had achieved with his Bible. Perhaps, after putting everything he had into his great printing invention, Johannes had lost his motivation.

Then, in January 1465, the archbishop of Mainz seems to have recognized Johannes's contributions. He gave Johannes the title "Gentleman of the Court" and a pension that allowed him an annual measure of grain, wine, and clothing. This did not make Johannes rich, but it meant that he could live out the last three years of his life in more comfort, before he passed away in 1468. However, at the time of his death, very few people had any idea what Johannes had achieved and how his great invention would change the world.

Fame After Death

Johannes's fame grew after his death. In 1504, he was credited with his invention in a book by Ivo Wittig, a professor at Mainz University. The first portrait of Johannes, likely an imaginary one, was not made until 1567, almost 100 years after his death, when he appeared in a famous biography of important Germans.

This statue of Johannes Gutenberg stands in Gutenberg Square in Strasbourg, France.

CHANGING THE WORLD

Johannes's invention of the printing press truly changed the world. Printers who had trained in his workshop went on to set up printing presses all over Europe, and gradually the invention was copied and spread. By 1500, there were around 1,000 printers in major cities across Europe, all using machines similar to Johannes's. They had produced more than eight million copies of books.

BOOKS AND BUSINESS

Before Johannes's printing press, books were expensive and only a privileged few could read. Most books were religious and written in Latin and Church leaders were the main owners of books. As books became affordable, people demanded works in their own languages, and they wanted a greater variety of books. Over the following centuries, printers began to publish poetry and travel books, books about art, math, science, or romance, and later even sheets or books of music. Newspapers were printed and bookstores and public libraries opened in cities. As the book trade began to flourish, so did industries related to it, such as papermaking, bookbinding, and writing.

Today, printing presses fill bookstores and libraries around the world with books full of information on every topic imaginable!

A NEW WAY OF THINKING

Until more people could read and afford books, they had relied on Church leaders for their understanding of the world. As books became less expensive, more people learned to read and information was distributed to a wide audience. Now, people could read about the world around them and begin to understand it in a new, more scientific way. They could decide what to think for themselves. This was not always popular with the Church and one pope even tried to **censor** printed books, but it was too late. So much knowledge was available to so many people, the world would never be the same again.

Modern printing presses, such as those used to print newspapers, have moved on since Johannes's first screw-type machines, but the power of the printed word is still just as powerful now as it was then.

The Word Is...

In April 1900, famous American writer Mark Twain wrote a letter in celebration of the opening of the Gutenberg Museum in Mainz. In it, he summed up the impact that Johannes and his invention of the printing press had made on the world when he said:

"What the world is today, good and bad, it owes to Gutenberg. Everything can be traced to this source, but we are bound to bring him homage ... for the bad that his colossal invention has brought about is overshadowed a thousand times by the good with which mankind has been favored."

TIMELINE

AD 600 The earliest printed paper scrolls are made in China using carved blocks of wood.

1045 Bi Sheng invents the first movable type in China. He made his movable type from wood and later clay, and each character he made could be reused.

1295 Marco Polo returns from Asia with news of woodblock printing that had spread around Europe.

1377 The first book printed with metal movable type is created in Korea.

The engraved portraits of Johannes were created long after his death and were based mainly on the artist's imagination.

1398 Johannes Gutenberg is born in Mainz, Germany.

1423 Block printing is used to print books in Europe.

1440 Johannes invents his wooden press, which uses movable metal type.

1455 Johannes publishes the first printed version of the Bible, which later becomes known as the *Gutenberg Bible*.

1455 Johannes loses a legal battle with Johann Fust and has to hand over his printing press and business.

1457 Fust and Schoeffer achieve the first color printing.

1468 Johannes dies and is buried in the Franciscan Church in Mainz.

1475 William Caxton brings the first printing press to England. The first book known to have been produced there was Chaucer's *The Canterbury Tales*.

1501 There are more than 1,000 print stores in Europe.

1501 Pope Alexander VI tries to censor printed books.

1525 The first printed music is published.

1605 The world's first printed newspaper is published in Strasbourg.

1690 The United States' first printed newspaper is published in Boston.

1710 Jacob Le Bron invents printing in color using three or four separate printing plates.

1725 Scottish goldsmith William Ged invents stereotyping, a process in which a whole page of type is cast in a single mold so that a printing plate can be made from it.

1800 British scientist Charles Stanhope builds the first printing press entirely out of iron.

1811 Friedrich Koenig invents a steam-powered printing press that could print copies faster than ever before.

1839 Electricity is used to run a printing press.

1844 US inventor Richard Hoe invents the Lightning Press, which was faster than the old flatbed press because it placed the type on a revolving cylinder.

1865 William Bullock invents the web offset printing press, in which paper is fed into a printing press on a continuous roll and printed on both sides.

1880 The first photographs are printed in newspapers.

1904 Ira Rubel invents offset litho printing, a method used to print images from a rotating rubber drum.

1946 Frenchmen René Alphonse Higonnet and Louis Marius Moyroud invent the Photon phototypesetter, which uses light and photographic paper for typesetting and is used to print large advertising posters.

1957 The first book to be entirely phototypeset is printed.

1971 Gary Starkweather invents the laser printer.

1971 Michael S. Hart sets up Project Gutenberg, a volunteer-run organization to digitize and archive cultural works, to encourage the creation and distribution of eBooks. Project Gutenberg is the world's oldest digital library.

1977 Ichiro Endo invents the inkjet printer, a printer in which the characters are formed by tiny jets of ink.

1984 Bob Doyle invents desktop publishing, in which a printer is linked to a desktop computer, with special software.

1984 Charles W. Hull invents the first working 3D printer.

1990 Tim Berners-Lee invents the Internet, or World Wide Web.

2015 3D printers can print and make parts for jets, toys, jewelry, guitars, buildings, and even limbs for people!

GLOSSARY

alloy A metal made from a mixture of different metals.

casting Forming by pouring hot metal (or wax) into a mold.

censor To examine books, letters, and other documents, in order to find and remove things that are considered offensive or harmful to society.

characters Written or printed letters, numbers, or symbols.

guildsmen People who were members of a guild. Guilds were formed of people who worked in the same business to protect their interests and maintain standards.

illuminated manuscripts Handwritten texts decorated with colorful initial letters, borders, and illustrations.

mint A factory where coins are made.

molds Hollow shapes into which a fluid or soft substance is placed to create particular shapes when it hardens.

monks Male members of a religious community who live by strict rules.

movable type A way of making and putting together individual pieces of type into groups, forming a printing surface.

pilgrim A person who travels to a sacred place for religious reasons.

plague A deadly disease that could spread quickly.

pope The leader of the Catholic Church.

printing frame A frame into which type blocks are arranged to print from.

scribes People who copied documents by hand.

type A small metal or wooden block with a raised surface in the shape of a character, used for printing.

vellum A type of paper made from the skin of a calf.

FOR MORE INFORMATION

Books

Childress, Diana. *Johannes Gutenberg and the Printing Press* (Pivotal Moments in History). Minneapolis, MN: Twenty First Century Books, 2008.

Hiller, Sandra J. *The Life of a Colonial Printer* (Jr. Graphic Colonial America). New York, NY: PowerKids Press, 2013.

Melchisedech Olsen, Kay. *Johann Gutenberg and the Printing Press* (Inventions and Discovery). Mankato, MN: Capstone Press, 2006.

Rumford, James. *From the Good Mountain: How Gutenberg Changed the World*. New York, NY: Flash Point, 2012.

Vander Hook, Sue. *Johannes Gutenberg: Printing Press Innovator* (Publishing Pioneers). Minneapolis, MN: ABDO Publishing Company, 2009.

Yomtov, Nel. *How the Printing Press Changed History* (Essential Library of Inventions). Minneapolis, MN: Essential Library, 2015.

Websites

Due to the changing nature of Internet links, PowerKids Press has developed an online list of websites related to the subject of this book. This site is updated regularly. Please use this link to access the list: **www.powerkidslinks.com/ithtw/gutenberg**

INDEX